HI THERE!

I'M CHRIS BARTON...

I'm an author of books for kids, and a big part of my job is visiting schools and talking to students.

And here's Ernie. A big part of his job is greeting me when I get home.

ERNIE

There are two questions that I'm asked a lot:

How do you make your books?

Are you ever going to write a book about your dog?

I can answer both of those at the same time. Ready? Here goes . . .

HOW TO make A BOOK (about my DOG)

WRITTEN BY CHRIS BARTON

ILLUSTRATED BY SARAH HORNE

MILLBROOK PRESS

MINNEAPOLIS

IF I'M MAKING A NONFICTION PICTURE BOOK ABOUT MY DOG, ERNIE, I'LL NEED A LOT OF HELP.

Not just from Ernie. And not just from the illustrator.

Picture books are created by a whole team of people whose names don't all appear on the cover.

At the very beginning of the process, though, it mostly is just me— just me, and lots of research.

That's true even when I'm working on a book about my own dog. Sure, I know Ernie pretty well, and I can tell you a lot about him:

· What he's good at (playing hide-and-seek)

· Whether he likes to swim (not at all)

· How he looks when I walk him (crooked, as if his back end is trying to see around his front)

Looking at photos and videos of Ernie will help me remember other things. But I'm not the only one with information about him.

I'll ask other members of my family, his veterinarian, the people who fostered Ernie before we adopted him, and even someone at the animal shelter where Ernie stayed before being rescued.

LOVE ERNIE!

WHAT ABOUT...

REMEMBER WHEN ERNIE MET MY CAT?

THIS, THAT, AND THE OTHER...

REMEMBER WHEN...

I HATE ERNIE!

Librarians can help too.
Maybe I'll visit a dog museum as well.

Why so much research about my own dog?

Well, there's a big difference between
how I introduce Ernie to a neighbor—

and the care I take with getting the facts right for a book about him:

TESTS REVEALED THAT ERNIE IS MOSTLY CHIHUAHUA and MINIATURE POODLE, PLUS DACHSHUND AND PART TERRIER, ALONG WITH A MIX OF OTHER BREEDS.

Even when I already know a subject well, I do plenty of research using many resources. My goal is always to understand my subject deeply so that I can explain it simply— and accurately.

SPANIEL

GREYHOUND

POMERANIAN

POODLE

FRENCH BULLDOG

DACHSHUND

ERNIE

Next, I'll start writing about Ernie. Maybe an idea of what to say will come to me suddenly while I'm walking him. (That happens often.)

Or maybe the words will take shape only after I sit down and set my mind to writing this story. (That happens a lot too.)

I GET IDEAS

← ON THE ROAD, AT THE HOTEL.

COOKING

AT MY DESK

Writing—and inspiration for what to write—can happen anywhere, anytime. That's why I usually keep a little notebook in my pocket.

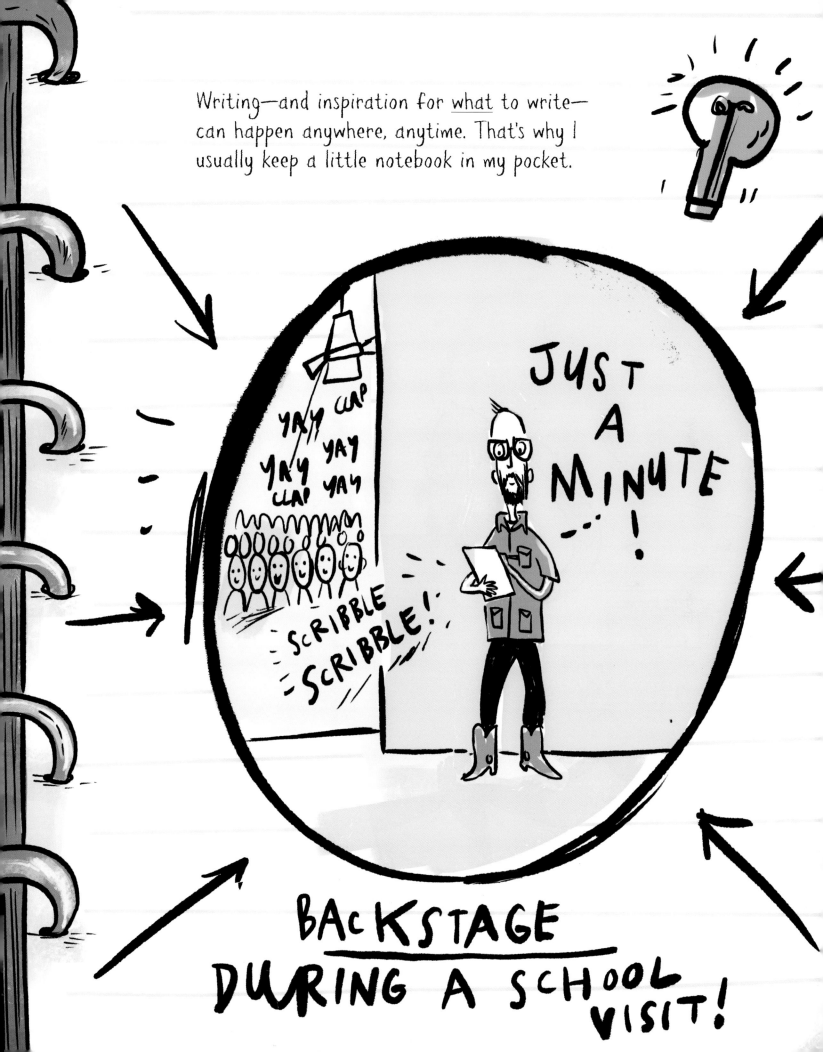

Sooner or later, I'll type up my manuscript about Ernie on my computer. I might read it out loud to a friend. Even then, what I have written might not be all that good.

But that's OK. Every story I write needs to be rewritten. This one is no different.

GRRR!

CHRIS'S IDEA FACTORY (HIS BRAIN)

A BOOK ABOUT MY DOG.

LANDS ON THE DESK OF CHRIS'S AGENT

OOO... LET ME PUT YOU BOTH ON HOLD...

A BOOK ABOUT MY DOG

OOO... I LOVE THIS!

AGENT SENDS TO EDITOR

A BOOK ABOUT MY DOG

THEN...

When I feel pretty good about the revised manuscript, I let my agent know. Like I said, picture book-making takes a team, and she's one of the first members of Team Ernie.

My agent will share the manuscript with someone who works for the publishing company that's going to turn my story into an actual book. And that person is my editor.

Editors do many things, but one of the most important is to help decide what books their company should publish.

They also get to share the good news—in great detail— with authors' agents. And they help those authors make their stories as good as they can be.

EXCELLENT!

GREAT OK...

Now, my editor might love what I've written so far about Ernie, and she may point out her favorite parts of the manuscript. But she will also see ways that I can improve what I've written.

In other words, it's time to revise some more!

MORE DRAFTS

BACK TO THE EDITOR FOR THE THUMBS-UP

Once my editor and I are both happy with the text—it isn't perfect, but it's pretty close to finished—we need someone to create the pictures.

I don't choose the illustrator, and neither does my editor. The actual choice of who the illustrator will be belongs to the art director.

The art director will want to pick someone whose style fits with my writing, who knows a lot about the subject, and who can draw or paint Ernie well.

After discussing candidates with the editor, with others at the publishing company, and maybe even with me, she'll come up with her top choice of illustrator.

The art director lets that artist's agent know about the opportunity to illustrate a book about Ernie.

If the artist and their agent want to join the team, and everybody's schedules line up, we've got ourselves an illustrator!

Sarah Horne says yes to illustrating the book. She and I live nearly five thousand miles apart, and we've never met.

Sarah will read my text all the way through. Then she'll reread it bit by bit, sketching as she goes.

Have I written something silly? She might use a wild style to reflect that. Are my words more thoughtful? She might take a calmer approach to match the mood of my writing.

To figure out what to show, Sarah uses her imagination, but she can also work from images or other guidance provided by the art director.

When Sarah has made sketches for the whole book, she'll share those with the rest of us on Team Ernie.

We'll provide feedback—comments about what we love and questions about parts we're not so sure about.

I might also tell her something about Ernie that I forgot to mention before, like the fact that he sometimes plays piano (though not very well).

After that, Sarah draws the final book by hand with pen and ink. Then she'll use digital tools to add color and texture.

That's right: the pencil marks and brushstrokes you see might have been made with a computer.

All the while that we're making a book about my dog, there are a bunch of questions that our team needs to answer.

Questions such as

WHAT?

WHEN?

WHEN?

What is our budget, and how can we make the best book possible with that amount of money? How much should the finished book cost?

When do we want the book to be published?

When does the text need to be final?

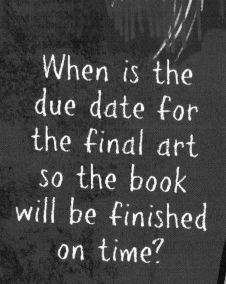

WHEN?

WHEN?

When is the due date for the final art so the book will be finished on time?

When will someone throw my squeaky carrot?

turn the page.

WILL WE INCLUDE PHOTOGRAPHS?

If so, whose permission do we need, and how do we acknowledge them?

Photos of Ernie © The Pet Gal

Do the book's title and cover get the attention of readers, give them a clear sense of what this book is about, and make them want to read it?

hmmm...

A BOOK ABOUT MY DOG

DO WE HAVE SOME **COLORS** THAT NEED TO BE MADE LIGHTER OR DARKER?

ANY IMAGES That need to BE DIGITALLY TWEAKED?

Are all the words speled right, and is the text punctuated correctly!

DID I REMEMBER TO WALK ERNIE?

Have the illustrator and I looked at the final version of the book?
Have we looked at the really final version?
hMM...
PROOFS
hMM....
PROOFS
Have we looked at the seriously, we mean it, this-is-the-last-chance final version?

So now we're ready for the
book to go to the printer, right?

RIGHT?

While the books are being printed, let's talk about software. Lots of different types of computer programs are used to make books.

WORD PROCESSING
SOFTWARE

ILLUSTRATION
SOFTWARE

BOOK DESIGN
SOFTWARE

SCHEDULING
SOFTWARE

DATABASE
SOFTWARE

ERNIE SOFTWARE

Ernie software?

Yes. Ernie soft here, and here, and here. (Sorry.)

After the books are printed, packed
into boxes, and shipped to the publisher's
warehouse, copies will be put into
different boxes—maybe with other titles.

Then those boxes will be sent off
to libraries and bookstores,

where someone will put one
particular copy onto a shelf,

where this book will wait for
the final member of our team:

YOU.

And if you like our nonfiction book about my dog, I've got a great idea for another book—one that Ernie himself could write:

HOW TO MAKE A SEQUEL (ABOUT MY HUMAN)

But that, of course, would be fiction.

THE END

HOW TO FIND OUT MORE ABOUT *HOW TO MAKE A BOOK (ABOUT MY DOG)* (AND EVERYTHING ELSE)

It doesn't matter how much or how little you already know about a subject when you start researching it; becoming more knowledgeable about something can feel great and be just as rewarding as it is challenging.

I think the most satisfying type of research is when you're focused on a topic that you're interested in—interested enough to write a book about it, or to consider studying it in school, or to pursue it purely for fun. For me, the hardest thing about researching is stopping my research. Ever hopeful that I'm *just one more* source away from learning the single most fascinating detail of the entire project, I always want to keep digging and digging.

If you're like me in this respect, reading a book such as *How to Make a Book (about My Dog)* may be only a first step in an inquiry into something you care about. In fact, a book like this might make you come up with new queries that you never considered before.

In that case, here are some further steps you can take:

Be specific.
Do you want to know more about *writing* books? *Illustrating* them? Agenting? Editing? Art directing? Publishing? Printing?

The clearer you are about which aspects of a subject you want to research, the better you'll be able to ask for the information you want. This can also help limit the amount of information you receive that you don't need.

Make sure you think about synonyms or other common names for the aspects that interest you. For instance, you might want to research "writers," "authors," *and* "novelists."

Look for glossaries.
There's a good chance that someone who is knowledgeable and trustworthy has shared a list, with definitions, of terms relevant to the subject you want to research. A web search for, say, *publishing* and *glossary* can be helpful in two ways.

First, having those terms already explained in writing means that you don't have to memorize them. You can just refer to the glossary when a source of information about your topic uses a term you don't know. Over time, you'll get familiar with the important ones.

Second, whoever provided that glossary might be a terrific source of additional information about your subject. What else can you learn from them?

Identify the experts.

Besides compilers of glossaries, there are other types of experts that might be useful to you.

- Groups. We're talking associations and organizations, also known as societies, institutes, councils, and guilds. There's a good chance that at least one such group—perhaps even located nearby—provides reliable information about your subject to other people in that field or to the public.

- Museums and archives. Whatever the field or topic, if even just a few people are passionate about it, there might well be at least one museum or archive dedicated to it, with exhibits and other information available in person or online.

- Authors, podcasters, and filmmakers. As you know, when someone is really into a subject, they might devote a big chunk of their life to writing about it for books (or magazines, or newspapers, or websites). Or recording themselves talking about it. Or making a documentary movie or TV show about it. You can't trust *everyone* who has that sort of passion, but many of them are careful to get their facts right and to share where they got their information. They may not have exactly what you're seeking, but they can help point the way forward.

Ask a librarian.

Librarians know so much about how to help people like you and me find the information we need, even if we don't know what it is. And the best ones are experts at using the single most powerful research tool: the question.

The question is the perfect combination of humble acceptance that something is not known and patient confidence that an answer can be found. (Why else would you ask?) There's one question in particular that I urge you to keep in mind no matter whether you're getting information from a representative of an association, a curator at a museum, an author, or a librarian.

When someone has been helpful, thank them—and ask, "Is there *just one more* source that you'd recommend?"

GOOD LUCK GETTING STARTED ON YOUR RESEARCH, AND HERE'S HOPING YOU NEVER WANT TO STOP!

TIMELINE OF MAKING THIS BOOK

Kids sometimes ask me, "How many books can you write in a day?" My answer surprises them: It usually takes four and a half or five years between the day I start working on a story idea and the day the book is available in schools and libraries and bookstores. (And that's assuming a story of mine *does* get turned into a book; many of my stories never do.) Sometimes, it takes less than three years, but one book of mine took fourteen. Along the way, I've learned how important it is not just to care about the book I'm trying to create but also to love the process of getting there. If you're going to be in a process for a long while, you'll be much happier if you find joy and satisfaction along the way. With this book, I certainly did.

Photo courtesy Chris Barton

8 years, 2 months before publication (BP): Chris Barton and his family adopt Ernie through Austin Dog Rescue.

5 years, 9 months BP: While writing his book about the use of dazzle camouflage on ships during World War I, Chris experiments with a version called *How to Write a Book about Dazzle Ships*. Editor gently suggests that this approach might be "a better fit for a simpler topic. Something like: How to Write a Book about a Dog."

3 years, 3 months BP: Chris emails Editor to ask if she'd be interested in a nonfiction picture book about how a book is made, mentioning he often gets asked about that process during his school visits.

2 years, 8 months BP: Editor brings Chris's outline and sample text for *How to Make a Book (about My Dog)* to an acquisitions meeting. The group says yes! (Chris usually has to write a complete manuscript before this happens, so he is especially excited by this news. Plus, he'll get to write about Ernie!)

2 years, 7 months BP: Editor sends an offer to Chris's agent for the manuscript, and they negotiate contractual details.

2 years, 3 months BP: Chris drives from his home in Texas to Minnesota to visit the offices of Lerner Publishing Group. As part of his research process, he interviews the editor and art director along with the publicist, a premedia operator, a production designer, a typesetter, the digital product manager, the purchasing manager, a customer service representative, the warehouse manager, the marketing director, the editor in chief, the publisher, and the publisher's dog, Percy.

LAST, BUT NOT LEASHED!

Photo courtesy Chris Barton

2 years, 2 months BP: Chris sends Editor a complete manuscript (well, except for the part about the illustrator's process).

1 year, 10 months BP: Editor sends Chris initial comments on the manuscript, and he sends back a revision two days later. Art Director shares samples from portfolios of illustrators who might be a good fit for the book.

1 year, 9 months BP: Editor shares the manuscript with another editor, who makes some comments and suggestions, and shares these thoughts with Chris. Once again, Chris sends in a revision in two days.

1 year, 8 months BP: Art Director hires Sarah Horne to illustrate. Editor sends (mostly) final text to typesetting. Art Director decides what size the book will be, how many pages it will have, and chooses a typeface for the text (though this might change after the art director sees how the type looks with the art).

1 year, 7 months BP: Chris interviews Sarah about her illustration process so he can correctly describe it in what until now has been a blank spread in the middle of the book.

1 year, 2 months BP: Chris, Editor, and the sales and marketing departments decide what the book's final title will be. (Sometimes it changes completely from what the author first called the book. In the case of this book, everyone agreed that the title Chris had given it was exactly right.)

1 year BP: Sarah turns in sketches. Chris, Art Director, and Editor review them, and Art Director provides feedback.

11 months BP: Sarah turns in revised sketches and several cover sketches. Art Director provides any final notes for little tweaks that Sarah should make when creating the final art. Art Director also shares cover sketches with the cover review group and receives many opinions on what will make the best cover. (The orange needs to be even more orange!)

10 months BP: Sarah turns in the final cover art, and Art Director again shares it with the cover group. They agree it's excellent! But are Chris's cowboy boots too close to the word "TO"? Perhaps they are. Do we really need cowboy boots on the cover at all? Well, they are a fun touch . . .

9 months BP: Sarah turns in the final art. The team rejoices! After reviews by Editor and Chris, Art Director decides whether to request any changes. They also review the text and mark changes that will help it sound better, be more accurate, or fit better with what's being shown in the art.

Photo courtesy Danielle Carnito
Photo of Ernie in photo courtesy Chris Barton

7 months, 2 weeks BP: Chris, Sarah, and everyone else working on the book review the layout with the updated final art and full back matter in place.

7 months, 1 week BP: A proofreader reviews the layout to check spelling, grammar, punctuation, and consistency. Publisher sends information to wholesalers (companies that sell books to bookstores and libraries) and online stores so they will be able to sell the book.

7 months BP: A premedia operator makes any necessary digital changes to the art, such as fading backgrounds behind the text so it will be easy to read.

6 months, 3 weeks BP: Chris and Sarah review the final layout. Art Director decides what color paper to use for the endsheets (the solid-colored pages that are glued to the inside of the front and back cover).

6 months, 2 weeks BP: Chris, Sarah, and everyone on the team reviews the seriously, we mean it, this-is-the-last-chance final version of the layout.

6 months, 1 week BP: The print buyer sends the final jacket, cover, and interior layout files to the printer. The premedia operator creates an ebook PDF.

6 months BP: The printer prints the cover, jacket, and pages of the book. To make the hard cover, a machine glues boards to the printed covers, and the cover art is wrapped around the edges of the boards. The printer folds and trims the pages and sews them together to make what's known as a book block. To attach the cover to the interior pages, the book block is glued into the spine, and the endsheets are glued down to the boards.

5 months BP: Early copies of the book are sent to reviewers so that bookstore and library buyers will be able to find out about the book and order it.

2 months BP: Finished books arrive in the warehouse.

3 weeks BP: Book shipments to wholesalers and other customers begin.

Publication Day: HOORAY! People can buy and read and share this book—yes, the very book you are reading right now!

For Karen Blumenthal, her excellent books,
and her excellent dog, Franklin
—C.B.

For Hazel
—S.H.

Millbrook Press™
An imprint of Lerner Publishing Group, Inc.
241 First Avenue North
Minneapolis, MN 55401 USA

For reading levels and more information, look up this title at www.lernerbooks.com.

Edited by Carol Hinz. Designed by art director Danielle Carnito.
Main body text set in PencilPete.
Typeface provided by JoeBob Graphics.
The illustrations in this book were created in Indian ink with a dip pen. Color and texture finished
in Photoshop.

Library of Congress Cataloging-in-Publication Data

Names: Barton, Chris, author. | Horne, Sarah, 1979– illustrator.
Title: How to make a book (about my dog) / written by Chris Barton and illustrated by Sarah Horne.
Description: Minneapolis, MN : Millbrook Press, [2021] | Audience: Ages 6–10 | Audience: Grades 2–3 |
    Summary: "Find out how books are made in this entertaining and engaging exploration of how to
    make a nonfiction picture book about author Chris Barton's real-life dog, Ernie"
    —Provided by publisher.
Identifiers: LCCN 2020053003 (print) | LCCN 2020053004 (ebook) | ISBN 9781541581289 |
    ISBN 9781728430911 (ebook)
Subjects: LCSH: Authorship—Juvenile literature.
Classification: LCC PN159 .B36 2021 (print) | LCC PN159 (ebook) | DDC 808.02—dc23

LC record available at https://lccn.loc.gov/2020053003
LC ebook record available at https://lccn.loc.gov/2020053004

Manufactured in the United States of America
1-47327-47954-4/1/2021